101 Amazing Things to Do in Singapore

© 2018 101 Amazing Things

All rights reserved. No part of this publication may be reproduced, distributed, or transmitted in any form or by any means, including photocopying, recording, or other electronic or mechanical methods, without the prior written permission of the publisher, except in the case of brief quotations embodied in critical reviews and certain other noncommercial uses permitted by copyright law.

Introduction

So you're going to Malaysia and/or Singapore, huh? You are so very lucky! You are sure in for a treat because this part of the world is one of a kind. You'll be treated to delicious treats, epic amounts of nature, incredible parties, wonderful shopping opportunities, and loads more coolness.

This guide will take you on a journey from the major places like Singapore, Kuala Lumpur, Penang, Ipoh, Melaka, the Cameron Highlands, Langkawi, Perhentian Islands, and more.

In this guide, we'll be giving you the low down on:
- the very best things to shove in your pie hole, from cheap food halls in Singapore's Little India through to super fancy restaurants in Kuala Lumpur
- incredible festivals, whether you would like to party hard to electronic music in the middle of a rainforest, or attend a festival dedicated to traditional dance
- the coolest historical and cultural sights that you simply cannot afford to miss like ancient mosques and temples, as well as world class museums

- the most incredible outdoor adventures, whether you want to have a white water rafting adventure, or you fancy getting up close to crocodiles
- where to shop for authentic souvenirs so that you can remember your trip forever
- the places where you can party like a local and make new friends
- and tonnes more coolness besides!

Let's not waste any more time – here are the 101 most amazing, spectacular, and cool things not to miss in Malaysia & Singapore!

First up, it's Singapore...

1. Eat Chicken Rice at the Maxwell Food Centre

Singapore is definitely not one of the cheapest places for budget travellers, but unless you want to eat in sit-down restaurants every night there is no reason why you can't stick to your budget. The city is brimming full of food centres, and one of the best loved is the Maxwell Food Centre, close to Chinatown. Chicken rice is a typical Singaporean dish, and it's what you should eat here – a delicious piece of chicken cooked in stock and served with fluffy rice.

(1 Kadayanallur Street)

2. Get Close to Animals at the River Safari

For an experience that will connect you with the nature of south-east Asia, a trip to the River Safari is huge amounts of fun. The rainforest setting represents 10 different ecosystems from around the world, including the River Nile, the Yangtze River, the Amazon, the Tundra, and more. There's a selection of gorgeous animals inside the park, such as anacondas, electric eels, giant otters, Chinese alligators, and Giant Pandas.

(80 Mandai Lake Road; www.riversafari.com.sg)

3. Learn to Love Durian at the Wonderful Fruit Enterprise

Durian might just be the most divisive fruit in the world. It has been nicknamed the stinky fruit, and while some people say it tastes like rotten onion custard other people totally swear by its deliciousness. With so many different opinions, you have to find out for yourself, and the place to do this is at the Wonderful Fruit Enterprise, where there are many durian sellers.

(147 Sims Ave)

4. Have a Fun Filled Day at Universal Studios Singapore

Of course, when you visit a new country it's a great idea to absorb yourself in the culture of the place, but you also need to set aside to have some major fun, and when you want to have a day of family fun in Singapore, Universal Studios is the place to be. At Universal Studios, you and the kids can ride on all kinds of roller coasters, enjoy 3D motion rides, and enjoy one of the greatest theme parks in Asia.

(8 Sentosa Gateway; www.rwsentosa.com/Homepage/Attractions/UniversalStudiosSingapore)

5. Get Back to Nature in the Singapore Botanic Garden

At first glance, it might seem as though Singapore is a concrete jungle, and while it's true that there are places where Singapore is really quite built up, that's only a first impression and there's actually quite a few places to immerse yourself in greenery. Singapore Botanic Gardens is just one such place. This 156 year old tropical garden is filled with delights, such as an orchid garden, a rainforest, and a ginger garden.

(1 Cluny Road; www.sbg.org.sg)

6. Have a Day of Learning at the National Museum of Singapore

If you fancy learning something new on your trip to Singapore, the National Museum is a must visit place. The museum dates all the way back to 1849, and as it's been building its collection since then, it's a place to get a really comprehensive schooling in the country. You'll get to see artefacts that date all the way back to the 14th century, as well as a number of contemporary collections that focus on film, fashion, and food.

(93 Stamford Road; http://nationalmuseum.sg)

7. Have an Artsy Day at the Singapore Art Museum

When you think of countries around the world that are renowned for their strong arts culture, it's unlikely that Singapore would be the first country that springs to mind. With that said, we don't think that art buffs will be disappointed on a trip to the city state, particularly if they visit the Singapore Art Museum. Housed in a restored 19th century mission school, this gallery contains contemporary works from Southeast Asia and Singapore.

(1 Bras Basah Road; www.singaporeartmuseum.sg)

8. Be Stunned by the Buddha Tooth Relic Temple

When you think of Buddhist temples, you probably think of ancient places that extend back for centuries, but while the Buddha Tooth Relic Temple was only built in 2007, we still think that it's pretty darn impressive to say the least. The highlight of a visit to this temple has to be checking out the two metre tall solid gold stupa that sits on the top floor of the temple's four storeys. There's also a museum inside to get to grips with Buddhism in Singapore.

(28 S Bridge Road; www.btrts.org.sg)

9. Dance Til You Drop at Zouk Nightclub

Yes, Singapore is a Muslim country where there is a high tax on alcohol, but this does not mean that you can't find some happening parties and local people who love to throw down. For a night out on the town, we think there's no better place to dance your socks off than at Zouk nightclub. This is a club that attracts international DJs, and has a mixed crowd of local youngsters, expats, and travellers as well.

(3C River Valley Road, #01-05, The Cannery;
http://zoukclub.com)

10. Cycle Around the Ketam Mountain Bike Park

While it's true that Singapore is best known for its shopping and food, if you are the outdoorsy type, you still have the opportunity to get active while you're in the country, and where better to raise your adrenaline than at the Ketam Mountain Bike Park? This 45 hectare park has 10 kilometres of biking trails, and the tracks are very impressive considering that international biking competitions are held there.
(Pulau Ubin)

11. Visit the Gorgeous Sri Mariamman Temple

For such a small country, Singapore has incredible cultural and religious diversity with many religious buildings. One of the most special is the Sri Mariamman Temple, which is Singapore's oldest Hindu temple dating all the way back to 1827 when the East India company developed a presence in Singapore. The temple has been built in the South Indian Dravidian style with lots of adornments such as sculptures and Hindu deities.
(244 South Bridge Road; www.smt.org.sg)

12. Take a Ride on the Singapore Flyer

Singapore is a beautiful place but you can only appreciate Singapore from a certain perspective when you view it by walking the streets. To get a killer view of Singapore, you simply have to take a ride on the Singapore Flyer, which at the time of being constructed was the largest Ferris Wheel in the whole world. It reaches a height of 550 feet so you'll get a stellar view of Singapore and the coast beyond.

(30 Raffles Avenue; www.singaporeflyer.com)

13. Drink a Singapore Sling in Its Birthplace

Although Singapore is a Muslim country with a pretty high tax on alcohol, this hasn't stopped the country from creating its own delicious cocktail, the Singapore Sling. This cocktail was created in the bar of the Raffles hotel by a Hainanese bartender in the early 20th century. The Singapore Sling is a fruity delight with a mix of gin, cherry liqueur, Cointreau, Benedictine, Grenadine, pineapple juice, lime juice, and bitters. For the authentic experience, head to Raffles Hotel for one of your own.

(1 Beach Road; www.raffles.com/singapore)

14. Shop Til You Drop on Orchard Street

If you love shopping you will love Singapore. This country is truly a shoppers' paradise, and as well as all of the many malls, somewhere where we like to put a dent in our wallets is along Orchard Street. This street spans 2.2 kilometres, so there are plenty of fashion boutiques and other stores to explore. Walk along this street and you'll have the opportunity to explore all of the brands that you know and love, such as Hugo Boss, Cartier, Alexander Wang, and many many more.

(www.orchardroad.org)

15. Cook Singaporean Dishes at Cookery Magic

While you're in Singapore, you are bound to fill your stomach with all kinds of delicious dishes, but how much better would it be if you knew how to make Singaporean food from scratch so that you could impress your friends with your cooking skills when you get home? Well, you have the opportunity to learn at Cookery Magic. You'll create yummy stuff like chicken stay, fish curry, chilli crab, laksa, and more.

(117 Fidelio St; http://cookerymagic.com)

16. Explore the Gardens By the Bay

While there is certainly a lot of concrete and many buildings and malls all over Singapore, there are some green spaces as well, and no doubt the most popular of these is the Gardens by the Bay, 250 acres of land next to the Marina Reservoir. There are many different gardens to explore, so whether you want to stroll through a cloud forest, a rainforest, or a Mediterranean landscape, there will be something for you.

(18 Marina Gardens Dr; www.gardensbythebay.com.sg/en.html)

17. Say Hi to Sea Animals at the South East Asian Aquarium

Southeast Asia is home to an incredible amount of wildlife, but you shouldn't forget about all the incredible sea creatures that exist in the oceans of the region. If you don't fancy something quite as adventurous as scuba diving, you can still get up close to many sea animals at Singapore's South East Asian aquarium. Inside, there's more than 100,000 sea animals from 800 species, including hammerhead sharks, moray eels, fire shrimp, and more.

(8 Sentosa Gateway, S.E.A. Aquarium, Resorts World Sentosa; www.rwsentosa.com/Homepage/Attractions/SEAAquarium)

18. Learn Something New at the Asian Civilizations Museum

Singapore may be a small country, but it has some of the best museums to be found anywhere in Asia in our opinion, and one of the museum highlights is the Asian Civilizations Museum. This is one of the pioneering museums of pan-Asian culture, specialising in the material history of China, Southeast Asia, South Asia, and West Asia. Highlights from the collection include Chinese porcelain, Burmese Buddhist art, and Peranakan gold. *(1 Empress Pl; http://acm.org.sg)*

19. Take in the Views With a Cocktail at Lantern Bar

When you're in Singapore on a Friday night, and you would like to have a relaxed drink somewhere that has a killer view, you can't do much better than Lantern Bar. This gorgeous rooftop bar sits on top of the Fullerton Bay Hotel, and as you sip on cocktails you'll have an amazing view of the Marina Bay and its nightly light show. The rooftop also has a pool and a sundeck if you would like to top up your tan in the daytime.

(80 Collyer Quay; www.fullertonhotels.com/en/singapore/the-fullerton-bay-hotel/dine/lantern-rooftop-bar)

20. Chow Down on Chilli Crab at Hua Yu Wee Seafood

When in Singapore, it's time to eat and eat and then eat some more. One of the most scrumptious local dishes is called Chilli Crab, which consists of a fresh catch of crab that is coated in a sweet, spicy, and savoury tomato based sauce. There are plenty of places to chow down on this deliciousness, but we are particularly enamoured by Hua Wee Seafood, where the portion is generous and full of flavour.

(462 Upper East Coast Rd)

21. Escape to Kusu Island for the Day

If you fancy getting a little bit off the beaten track while you're in Singapore, it can be a great idea to take the ferry from the south coast to Kusu island, which translates as tortoise island. There is a lot to explore away from the mainland on Kusu, with the Da Bo Gang Temple, which is dedicated to the Chinese God of Prosperity, and swimming lagoons and beaches where you can simply have some fun in the sun.

22. Go Hiking in the Bukhit Timah Nature Preserve

It's true that Bukhit Timah Nature Reserve is not the largest of green spaces, but even thought it's small, the 400 acres close to the downtown area contain a whole lot of diversity, and there are 840 species of flowering species within the green space. When you simply want to take it easy and perhaps have a stroll, a hike, or a run with some fresh air, this is the place to be.

(Hindhede Dr; www.nparks.gov.sg/gardens-parks-and-nature/parks-and-nature-reserves/bukit-timah-nature-reserve)

23. Keep Kids Entertained at the Singapore Science Centre

Travelling with kids is a double edged sword. It's wonderful to provide them with lifelong memories and to allow them to explore different cultures, but it can also be a draining experience as kids have the need to be entertained all the time. With 850 exhibits spread across eight different galleries, and many of these interactive, there is plenty to explore. The observatory inside is also a highlight with stargazing sessions every Friday.

(15 Science Centre Road; www.science.edu.sg/Pages/SCBNewHome.aspx)

24. Check out Contemporary Art at 8Q SAM

If contemporary art is what does it for you, there are quite a few contemporary arts spaces around Singapore, and 8Q SAM is one of the best of these spaces. It's an annexe of the gargantuan Singapore Art Museum, and this is the place where you really get to see art work at its most cutting edge in the country. There's also an annual contemporary children's art exhibition.

(8 Queen St)

25. Eat at a Michelin Starred Restaurant, L'Atelier

When you are on holiday, it's time to really push the boat out and be indulgent, and what better way to get a little bit decadent than by reserving a table at a Michelin star restaurant? Lucky for you, Singapore has quite a few of these, and L'Atelier is a place that totally epitomises fine dining. This French restaurant has earned itself two

Michelin stars, and there is little wonder why. The foie gras custard is a must try.

(26 Sentosa Gateway, Hotel Michael;
www.rwsentosa.com/Homepage/Restaurants/CelebrityChefs/LAte lierdeJo%C3%ABlRobuchon)

26. Discover New Music at Neon Lights Festival

When you think of the world's best music festivals, you might not immediately think of Singapore, but if it's dancing away to live music that really does it for you, we think you'll be more than happy at the Neon Lights Festival. Because the sun shines all year round in Singapore, this festival adds some brightness to the month of November. Acts that have performed include Sigur Ros, Foals, Crystal Castles, and many more besides.

(www.neonlights.sg)

27. Take in a Show at the Victoria Theatre & Concert Hall

When you are stuck for something to do at the weekend in Singapore, be sure to check out the programme of the Victoria Theatre, which is one of the best performing arts centres in the city state. The concert venue is used as a performance space by the Singapore Symphony Orchestra, but you can catch many different kinds of performances from contemporary dance shows through to live jazz and lots more besides.

(9 Empress Pl)

28. Tuck Into an Indian Feast at the Tekka Centre

You can find many different types of food in Singapore, and if you fancy something different from the Singaporean classics it can be a great idea to head to Little India, which has many Indian eateries but also a massive food hall called the Tekka Centre. There's all kinds of Indian grub, but it's the mutton biryani and the roti with chicken curry that we come back for again and again. There are also plenty of veggie options.

(Bukit Tumah Road)

29. Get to Grips With Peranakan Culture at the Peranakan Museum

The Peranakan people are people who came from China to the Malaysia, Singapore, and Indonesia between the 15th

and 17th centuries. They have left and enduring legacy in Singapore and beyond, and the best place to get to grips with this of local history is at the Peranakan Museum. The museum is beyond comprehensive, and the galleries contain fascinating exhibits. You'll learn about the 12 day Peranakan Museum, how a Peranakan feast would have been with Nonya porcelain, arts and crafts like beadwork and textiles, and lots more.

(39 Armenian St; http://peranakanmuseum.org.sg)

30. Eat a Kaya Toast Breakfast at Chin Mee Chin Confectionary

It may not be the healthiest start to the day, but if you want to eat breakfast like a local Singaporean, you have to try kaya toast, which is basically chargrilled toast that is slathered with a local jam made from coconut and eggs. There are countless places to grab a plate of this in Singapore, but we are very fond of Chin Mee Chin Confectionary, which has a really charming old-school feel.

(204 E Coast Road)

And now on to Malaysia…

31. Get Back to Nature in the Kuala Lumpur Bird Park

There is plenty of nature to be explored when you are in Malaysia, and you can even find some green escapes in the capital city. When the honking cars get too much, simply make your way to the oasis that is the Kuala Lumpur Bird Park where there are more than 3000 birds, and 90% of these are local to Malaysia. Inside the park, you can spot birds as beautiful and diverse as crowned pigeons, blue peacocks, and even ostriches

(Jalan Cenderawasih, Tasik Perdana, Kuala Lumpur; www.klbirdpark.com)

32. Enjoy Lazy Beach Days on the Perhentian Islands

When you think of beach destinations in southeast Asia, your mind would probably wander to the islands of Thailand or the Philippines, but there is also ample opportunity to catch some lazy beach time in Malaysia, and one of the most gorgeous places for this is certainly the Perhentian Islands. There's a range of beaches on the island, so whether you would prefer to laze in a secluded spot with a book or you'd like to try some adventurous watersports, these islands are bound to satisfy.

33. Cook Local Food in a Malay Village

Something that you will soon discover on your trip to Malaysia is that the food is delicious and extremely diverse. Of course, you should fill your stomach with as much of it as you possibly can, but even better is learning how to cook Malaysian food yourself – that way you can eat it whenever the fancy takes you. There are many cooking schools but we love Bayan Indah, which exists in a Malay village not too far from the capital. You'll cook traditional things like laksa in a beautiful setting.

(Jalan Palimbayan Indah 4, Kampung Sungai Penchala; www.bayanindah.com)

34. Geek Out Over Cameras in Penang

There is plenty to keep museum buffs and art buffs occupied around Malaysia, and one of the most overlooked but very charming museums is the Camera Museum in George Town, Penang. Across the museum,

you will encounter over 1000 cameras and camera related accessories from the days when, believe it or not, people didn't have smartphones to take their photos with. We love the pin hole camera room, and the dark room that gives you a great idea about processing photos
(www.thecameramuseumpenang.com)

35. Party Til the Early Hours at Havana Club

Although Malaysia is a Muslim country where the prices of alcohol are on the expensive side, it's definitely a place where you can find a party if you fancy it, and especially in KL. Havana Club is the kind of place where you can dance all night and make local friends, but if you would like to have more of an early night they also serve up some great comfort food like gumbo and other Cajun cuisine.
(Changkat Bukit Bintang, Bukit Bintang, KL;
http://havanakl.com)

36. Get Close to Turtles in Cherating

One of the most special things that you can do in Malaysia is get really close to some of the wildlife, and in Malaysia you can do better than seeing animals in cages in zoos.

The Turtle Wildlife Sanctuary in Cherating is a place to get close to turtles in a natural habitat. Something very special about this place is their camping facilities. Turtles are more active at night time, so camping will give you the chance to see them hatching from eggs, and landing on the rockeries.
(Bukit Cherating, 26080 Balok, Pahang)

37. Hike up Penang Hill
When you are on the island of Penang, there are tonnes of cultural experiences, particularly in the Georgetown area, but that is not the beginning and end of the Penang experience, and if you are something of an adventurer you can also enjoy some hiking up Penang hill, which also contains local botanic gardens and many areas of natural beauty. If you don't want to get out of breath, there's also a train that can take you all the way to the top!
(www.penanghill.gov.my/index.php/en)

38. Visit the Buddhist Temple Complex of Kek Lok Si
Although Malaysia is a Muslim country, this doesn't mean that you can't find other religious buildings around the country, and some very impressive ones at that. The Kek

Lok Si temple is the largest Buddhist temple in all of Malaysia, located on the island of Penang. This is a spectacularly impressive temple with a seven story pagoda that features 10,000 alabaster and bronze statues of the Buddha.

(1000-L, Tingkat Lembah Ria 1, 11500 Ayer Itam, Pulau Pinang; http://kekloksitemple.com)

39. Tuck Into Traditional Malaysian Laksa

One of the highlights of any trip to Malaysia is the food, and perhaps the most famous of all Malaysian food is laksa. You can pretty much find it in all local restaurants in every town and city across the country, so there really is no excuse not to slurp on lots of it. If you are unfamiliar with laksa, it's a hearty bowl of rice noodle soup that is flavoured with a spicy coconut based broth, and inside you'll typically find shrimp, cockles, and sometimes chicken

40. Hit a Few Golf Balls at the Royal Selangor Golf Club

Yes, there is lots to see and explore while in Malaysia, but there might be some times that you simply want to relax and unwind by hitting up a golf course, and you have quite a few options while in Malaysia. One of the most renowned courses in the country is the Royal Selangor Golf Club, and since it dates back to 1893 it's one of the oldest golf clubs to be found anywhere in Asia.
(www.rsgc.com.my)

41. Dance to Live Bands at Urbanscapes

If you want to feel the pulse of Malaysia's creative culture, it's imperative that you check out Urbanscapes, the country's longest running creative arts festival. This festival takes place across the end of April and the beginning of May, and is dedicated to showcasing the talents of local music artists and other types of performing artists. There's also a handful of international artists playing, with previous acts like Tame Impala and Rudimental. The festival is held annually in KL.
(http://urbanscapes.com.my)

42. Trek the Jungle Trails of Penang National Park

Malaysia is a country full of green spaces large and small, and, in fact, it is home to the smallest national park in the whole world: Penang National Park. But when you arrive at this park you will soon realise that size is not everything. Although it's a small space, the area features gorgeous low mangroves, hardwood trees, and rocky coastline, so it's a magnificent place to relax and simply immerse yourself in Malaysian beauty.

(Pejabat Taman Negara P. Pinang, Jalan Hassan Abbas, Balik Pulau)

43. Camp Next to the Chiling Waterfalls

There are numerous waterfalls to be found around Malaysia, and we think that one of the most stunning of these is the Chiling Waterfalls in Selangor. There are three waterfalls here, and a 3km trek along a gushing river to get to them, so there is plenty to explore. And if you fancy making your trip to the waterfall even more of an adventure, you'll be glad to know that there is a campsite close to the entrance so you can camp out under the stairs and then take your morning bath under the waterfall.

(44000 Kuala Kubu Bharu, Selangor)

44. Be Stunned by the Works at the Islamic Arts Museum

Kuala Lumpur is a city with a handful of incredible museums, but for our money the best of them all is the Islamic Arts Museum. This is well regarded as the largest and most comprehensive museum of Islamic art in southeast Asia with more than 7000 beautiful artefacts to explore. Some of the beautiful objects you'll find inside include gorgeous calligraphy inscribed pottery, local jewellery, textiles from the Islamic world, and lots more.
(Jalan Lembah Perdana, Tasik Perdana, Wilayah Persekutuan, Kuala Lumpur; www.iamm.org.my)

45. Party at the Rainforest World Music Festival

When you think about places in the world that are famous for their banging music festivals, it's very unlikely that Malaysia would be the first name that springs into your head, but actually there are quite a few festivals worth checking out in Malaysia. The Rainforest World Music Festival will make festival lovers very happy indeed. Set against the backdrop of the Borneo rainforest, there are music acts performing live from all over the world. It takes place in July each year.

(http://rwmf.net)

46. Sip on Decadent Cocktails at PS150

Alcoholic drinks tend to be on the expensive side on Malaysia, but when you need a drink you need a drink, and when that moment strikes, we like to sit back and relax with one (or five) of the cocktails at PS150 in Kuala Lumpur. With its bare brick walls and exposed pipes, you'd be forgiven for that you're in Berlin instead of southeast Asia, and it's a nice change if you want something different. Our favourite cocktail is the Pandan Flip, a pandan infused dark rum, with coconut bitters, and an egg yolk.

(150 Ground Floor, Jalan Petaling, Kuala Lumpur; www.ps150.my)

47. Indulge a Sweet Tooth With Some Apom Manis

Malaysian food isn't all slurpy noodles and curries, and fans of sweet treats are in for some culinary delight as well. One of our favourite sweet things to eat while in Malaysia is called Apom Manis, which are originally a Tamil food from south India that made its way to Malaysia thanks to the large Tamil population. These are small pancakes that have coconut milk in the batter to make them extra delicious. They should be light and crispy on the outside while squidgy in the middle.

48. Tuck Into a Traditional Nasi Lemak Breakfast

They say that breakfast is the most important meal of the day, and while in Malaysia why not take the opportunity to eat breakfast just like the local people do? Nasi Lemak is just the ticket. Now, when you see Nasi Lemak, you'd probably think of it as more of a dinner time meal, but this is very popular at the beginning of the day. It consists of rice cooked in coconut milk that is served with fried anchovies, peanuts, a hard boiled egg, and a spicy sauce.

49. Tour the Famous Petronas Towers

When you look into the cityscape of Kuala Lumpur you can often see the dominant twin skyscrapers that are the Petronas Towers. From 1998 to 2004, these buildings were the largest in the world, and they are still the biggest twin skyscrapers. There is a bridge that connects the two towers, and it is possible to purchase tickets to walk across the bridge, and take in the view of all of Kuala Lumpur from an incredible height.

(www.petronastwintowers.com.my)

50. Take a Ride on the Genting Skyway

There are many wonderful ways to explore Malaysia, and one of our favourite ways of all is by taking a ride on the Genting Skyway, a sky gondola that connects the Genting area that's a little north of the capital city. The journey on the gondola will take you up and down a beautiful mountain peak, so this is a great way of getting to know the natural landscapes of Malaysia but without any physical exertion whatsoever.

(www.rwgenting.com/getting-here/awana-skyway)

51. Visit a Temple Filled With Pit Vipers

There's certainly no shortage of temples around Malaysia, and while many of them are beautiful and great to visit, the most unique has to be the Snake Temple on the island of Penang. In fact, this temple is the only one of its kind in the whole world. The whole temple is filled with the smoke of burning incense and lots of pit vipers. There is no need to be too scared about visiting because the snakes have had their venom removed.

(Jalan Sultan Azlan Shah, Bayan Lepas Industrial Park, Penang)

52. Climb to the Top of Mount Kinabalu

If you are the kind of person who loves to get active while you're on holiday, then there are plenty of great hikes that you can try while you are in Malaysia. It's not an easy climb but we think that a climb to the top of Mount Kinabalu is particularly rewarding. This mountain is actually located in Malaysian Borneo, which is renowned for its landscapes. Most climbers take two days to get to the 4000 metre peak and back down again.

53. Get to Grips With Local History at the Baba Nyonya Heritage Museum

About 400 years ago, a great Chinese explorer called Admiral Cheng Ho brought Chinese settlers to the small Malaysian city of Melaka. It's these people of Chinese Straits origin that are also called the Baba and Nyonya, and

you can learn more about them at the Baba Nyonya Heritage Museum, also in Melaka. You can walk around the museum at any time by yourself, but we highly recommend the guided tours, which are delivered with personality and make you learn so much more.
(48-50, Jalan Tun Tan Cheng Lock, Melaka; http://babanyonyamuseum.com)

54. Create a Batik Painting at the Jadi Batek

Malaysia is a country that has many traditional handicrafts, and one of the most beloved of these is batik. Batik is essentially the process of wax resistant dyeing that is applied to cloth to create intricate patterns. The Jadi Batek gallery in Kuala Lumpur is a place where you can see many beautiful designs, but you'll also have the chance to create your own batik painting in one of their workshops.
(30, Jalan Inai, Imbi, 55100 Kuala Lumpur; www.jadibatek.com)

55. Relax at the Banjaran Hotsprings Retreat

There is so much to see, do, and explore in Malaysia, but sometimes all you want to do is relax, unwind, and feel the weight of the world fall from your shoulders in a beautiful setting. And that's when you book a few nights at the exceptional Banjaran Hotsprings Retreat in Ipoh. This is a very special place that brings luxury and wellness together in the most spectacular fashion. With waterfalls and natural hot springs on the premises, there's no better way to indulge.

(1 Persiaran Lagun Sunway 3, 31150 Ipoh; www.thebanjaran.com)

56. Visit the Boh Tea Plantations in the Hills

Malaysia is an extremely important place in the world for tea production, and you can find most of the tea plantations in a beautiful area with high altitude called the Cameron Highlands. There are many tea estates here that you can visit, and we think our favourite is the Boh Tea Estate. This plantation was opened all the way back in 1929 during the British colonial period, and it still operates today with a free tour through the factory to show you how the tea is processed.

(Boh Road Habu, 39200 Ringlet, Pahang; www.boh.com.my)

57. Eat Chicken Rice Balls in Melaka

Melaka is a small city with a hell of a lot to eat, but there is one dish that stands head and shoulders above the rest in this town: chicken rice balls. This is a really simple dish, it basically is what it says on the tin, but that does not prevent it from being totally delicious in any way whatsoever. Order a plate of this and you'll find soft, poached chicken that is perfectly moist served up with sticky rice balls and a soya sauce dip. You can find this treat all over Melaka, and a concentration of restaurants on Jonker Street.

58. See Orangutans in the Wild at Semenggoh Nature Reserve

There's a huge amount of wildlife to be found in Malaysia, and one of the most special places to visit to get close to animals in their natural habitat is the Semenggoh Nature Reserve in Kuching. This nature reserve is home to many native animals, but is best known for its population of orangutans, of which there are only about 25,000 left in the wild. The reserve does an incredible job of looking after these creatures, and it's truly heart warming to see them living as they should in the Malaysian jungle.
(https://sarawaktourism.com/attraction/semenggoh-nature-reserve)

59. Take a Canopy Walk at the Rainforest Discovery Centre

If you love nothing more than to immerse yourself in nature, we think that the Rainforest Discovery Centre is one of the best places for environmental education in the whole country. There are a number of attractions, including guided night time walks, and a plant discovery garden, but it's the canopy walk that steals the show. This is a 147 metre walkway that is raised 28 metres above the ground, and as you walk across, you'll have spectacular vistas of the whole rainforest.

60. Visit a Living Museum, the Sarawak Cultural Village

If you think that walking from one stuffy museum to another sounds totally boring, we think that the Sarawak Cultural Village might just be the museum that converts you. This is a living museum, and it does a fantastic job of bringing Sarawak's cultural heritage to life. There are 150 people living in the village who bring to life the cultures of native tribes. You'll get to witness them making handicrafts, cooking, putting on dances, and lots more besides.

(Damai Beach Resort, 93762, Kampung Budaya Sarawak; www.scv.com.my)

61. Take a Stroll Through the Penang Botanical Gardens

Penang is a place that is known for its quaint streets and for its delicious food, but there's also a good deal of nature to be found on the island, and if you're in the mood for some greenery, we would recommend a trip to the Penang Botanical Gardens. The original gardens were established all the way back in 1884, and contains many wonderful plants and trees in a mainly rainforest environment with orchids, spices, and many other treasures besides.

(673A, Jalan Kebun Bunga, Pulau Tikus, 10350 George Town, Pulau Pinang; http://botanicalgardens.penang.gov.my/index.php/en)

62. Explore the Limestone Caves of Niah National Park

Located in Malaysian Borneo, Niah National Park is not one of the largest parks of Malaysia but it's certainly one of the most impressive and popular. This is because it contains the Great Cave, which is one of the largest caverns anywhere in the world. It is possible to visit the caves inside this park without any guide, and you'll be surrounded by an abundance of bats, and you might even get to see some pre-historic cave paintings.

63. Indulge a Bibliophile at the Malacca Literature Museum

When you think of countries around the world that are famous for their literary works, Malaysia might not be the first country that springs to mind, but if you are a bibliophile, fear not, because there's a whole literary world to be explored at the Malacca Literature Museum. This museum pays specific attention to the history of writing and literature in Malaysia right from the period of the Melaka Sultanate and up to the present day.

(Jalan Kota, Bandar Hilir, 75000 Melaka; www.perzim.gov.my)

64. Check Out the Spiritual Sculptures of Mah Meri Cultural Village

There are some lovely islands off the mainland of Malaysia, but if you fancy visiting an island that's a little more off the beaten track, we think that Carey Island could be just what you are looking for. The main attraction here is the Mah Meri Cultural Village, where you will learn about the Mah Meri indigenous people and their beautifully intricate wood carvings, which they use for spiritual healing.

(Jln Kampong Orang Asli Sungai Bumbun, Kampung Manikavasagam, 42960 Pulau Carey; http://mmcv.org.my/web)

65. Have the Local Experience With Couchsurfing

As you travel around Malaysia, you are likely to stay in an assortment of hotels, hostels, and guesthouses, but if you fancy having more of a local experience with your accommodation then you should definitely take a look at the Couchsurfing website. The basic idea of the site is that local people offer up their spare beds or sofas at no cost to travellers. As well as being a way to save money, this is also a great way to have an authentic cultural exchange.

(www.couchsurfing.com)

66. Enjoy Communal Eating in Penang With Some Lok Lok

What exactly is Lok Lok we hear you cry? Well, it's actually not something specific to Malaysia but that's popular in many places in Asia, but it happens to be called Lok Lok in Malaysia and Penang specifically. Lok Lok is a communal hotpot. In the centre of a table you'd have bubbling pots of stock and gravy, into which you cook skewers of things like squid, shrimp, cockles, chicken, pork, mushrooms, and other vegetables. It's a lovely way to eat if you're with a group of people.

67. Purchase Prisoner Made Handicrafts From My Pride

In many ways, Malaysia is a very progressive country, and we think that the rest of the world could definitely take a leaf out of Malaysia's book when it comes to the way they treat prisoners. The Malaysian government is dedicated to providing inmates with vocational skills, and when in Malaysia it's possible to purchase products handmade by inmates under the My Pride brand. You can find these in many shops in the Klang valley area.

68. Be Stunned by the Beautiful Putra Mosque

Since Malaysia is a Muslim country, you can find lots of incredible mosques dotted around the country. One of the most impressive of these is the Putra Mosque, which you can find in the town of Putrajaya. What sets this mosque apart from others is its fairytale-like pink colour. The main dome and other smaller domes have been crafted from pink granite, and have all kinds of embellishments that make it something really beautiful to behold.

(Pusat Pentadbiran Kerajaan, 62502 Persekutuan, Wilayah Persekutuan Putrajaya; www.masjidputra.gov.my)

69. Take Home Some Pottery From Ayer Hitam

Malaysia is a country with many traditional handicrafts, and if it's pottery and ceramics that interest you, you should definitely think about making a trip to the town of Ayer Hitam, which totally specialises in the ceramic arts. You'll be able to find local potters and huge factory outlets alike, so you should have no problem finding something extra special to take home with you.

70. Visit a Chinese Clanhouse, Khoo Kongsi

A Chinese clanhouse is essentially a building in a foreign country that was built to support local Chinese communities. Since there is a large immigrant Chinese population in Malaysia, these can be found right over the country, but the most impressive of them is Khoo Kongsi in Penang. The building was constructed more than 650 years ago, and the lavish decorations of the house make it something that you can keep looking at for hours and always find something new.

(Cannon Square, George Town, 10450 George Town; www.khookongsi.com.my)

71. Try a Strange Malaysian Dessert, Cendol

Malaysia is definitely better known for its savoury classics than its sweet treats, but if you do have a sweet tooth, we don't think that Malaysia will disappoint you either. One of the most popular desserts in the country is cendol, and honestly, this dessert is plain weird, but it's also really good, and you need to try it at least once. Cendol combines sweetened shaved ice, pandan flavoured cold noodles, coconut milk, and sometimes there are some red beans floating around in there too.

72. Have a Meal to Remember at Babe in KL

If your idea of great vacation involves lots and lots of food, Kuala Lumpur is a destination that will not disappoint. But with so many restaurants to pick from, it can be hard to make any kind of decision. So let us recommend Babe. This restaurant prioritises fun dining over fine dining, but that's not to say the food is bad, because we think their Japanese tapas is all kinds of delicious. The cedar smoked jackfish and sumi squid are particularly special.

(Clearwater, Jalan Changkat Semantan, Bukit Damansara, 50490 Kuala Lumpur; http://babe.com.my)

73. Explore the Impressive Batu Caves

Malaysia is bursting full with all kinds of geographical wonders, and the Batu Caves, a series of limestone formations on the edge of Kuala Lumpur, are something that every visitor to the city simply has to explore. At the entrance you will find a stunning large Golden statue of a Hindu God. You can climb its 277 steps to reach the top, from which point you have an incredible view of all the surrounding vistas.

(www.malaysia.travel/en/nl/places/states-of-malaysia/selangor/batu-caves)

74. Stroll Through a Durian Orchard, Art & Garden

When you are in southeast Asia, something that you won't be able to escape is the famous (or should that be infamous?) durian fruit. Many local people say that this is the king of fruits, while other people would liken its taste to a cream of rotten onions. Well, if you would like a different perspective on the durian fruit, it can be a great idea to visit a durian orchard called Art & Garden on Penang. The orchard is home to a conceptual glass artist where you can also peruse his stunning installations.

(Jalan Tanjung Bungah, 11000, Pulau Pinang)

75. Be Wowed by the Giam Klimau Waterfall

Although Malaysia is probably best known for its cultural centres like Kuala Lumpur and Georgetown, there is still a huge amount to explore for nature lovers, you will simply have to get off the beaten track a little. A gushing waterfall is always impressive, and Giam Klimau might just be the best in the whole country. It is located about 85km away from a city called Miri in remote oil palm plantations. There is also a natural pool there for swimming.

76. Visit the Oldest Hindu Temple in Malaysia

Although Malaysia is officially a Muslim country, you can find some other stunning buildings of workshop dotted around the country. One of the most beautiful of these is called Sri Mahamariamman, the oldest Hindu temple in the country, which can be found in Kuala Lumpur. The temple was built in the 1860s, and its most stunning feature is a five tiered tower, which is decorated with depictions of the Hindu Gods, created by south Indian artisans.

(Jalan Tun H S Lee, City Centre, 50000 Kuala Lumpur)

77. Enjoy the Fun of the Sabah International Folklore Festival

If you find yourself in Malaysia during the month of August, something fun, entertaining, and educational that you won't want to miss is the Sabah International Folklore Festival. At this festival, the city of Sabah invites traditional dance troupes from all over the world to Malaysia to showcase their own dances and artistic expression.

78. Have a Magical Morning at the Penang Butterfly Farm

The Penang Butterfly Farm dates all the way back to 1986 and was one of the first tropical butterfly farms in the whole world. Since it opened, the butterfly farm has grown to a population of more than one thousand butterflies from over 120 species, and being surrounded by so many of these delicate creatures is a truly magical experience. This is an awesome place to take kids and get them interested in nature.

(Jalan Teluk Bahang, Teluk Bahang, 11050 Penang; http://entopia.com)

79. Indulge at a Malaysian Speakeasy, Private Room

Because Malaysia is a Muslim country, sometimes bar options can be limited, but if you do love to have a night out, we can heartily recommend stopping by Private Room in the capital city, Kuala Lumpur. Private Room is the city's very first speakeasy wine bar where you can feel the worries of the world slide from your shoulders. You'll also be glad to know that the bar is owned by a total of seven wine enthusiasts, so the drinks menu is sure to impress.

(Persiaran Zaaba, Taman Tun Dr Ismail, 60000 Kuala Lumpur)

80. Dive the Coral Reefs of Tioman Island

A great deal of Malaysia is surrounded by water, and this means that there are things to be explored within the water as well as on the land, and what better way of exploring those waters than with a scuba diving trip. For our money, the best place for a spot of diving in Malaysia is Tioman Island, and this is not least because of the spectacular coral reef that exists there. You'll have the chance to swim amongst the coral and the sea creatures.

81. Rock Out at Rock The World Malaysia

While many music festivals seem to cater to fans of electronic music these days, the alternative is Rock The World Malaysia, which as you have probably guessed is a festival that is organised with fans of guitar music in mind. While the festival manages to attract some rock talent from around the world, we think that the real appeal of the festival is having the chance to check out some of the Malaysian music talent. The festival takes place in December in KL.

82. Chow Down on Plenty of Rendang

The local people of Malaysia certainly do know how to eat, and if you enjoy filling your stomach with lots of spicy food, you may already be familiar with rendang, which is a spicy meat curry that is enjoyed all over Indonesia and Malaysia. You can find all different kinds of meats in a rendang, but beef is probably the most traditional. The thick sauce typically contains coconut, garlic, shallots, chilli, ginger, and lemongrass, and it packs a mighty punch.

83. Take a Ride on the Jungle Railway

There are many different ways to traverse the land of Malaysia, and one of our favourite ways has to be taking a ride on the Jungle Railway, which starts in Trumpat and winds its way through thick rainforest to reach Kota Bahru. At some points the jungle surrounding the train is so dense that the foliage scrapes against the train carriages on both sides to that you feel totally immersed in nature. You can only buy tickets on the same day.

84. Pick Strawberries in the Cameron Highlands

The Cameron Highlands is the best place in Malaysia for escaping the heat and humidity, and for cooling off a little in beautiful greenery. This part of the country is best known for its gorgeous tea plantations that thrive thanks to the cool temperatures that the altitude brings. But this part of Malaysia isn't just about tea, it's also a spot where a lot of strawberries are grown. The Big Red Strawberry Farm is a place where you can actually pick strawberries yourself and also eat lots of strawberry flavoured treats.
(Brinchang, 39000 Brinchang, Pahang;
http://bigredstrawberryfarm.com)

85. Shop at the Bustling Central Market in Kuala Terengganu

If you want to get to a know a country, you really have to immerse yourself in its market culture. This is particularly important in southeast Asia, and one of the greatest markets in Malaysia is the Central Market in Kuala Terengganu. Now this isn't the kind of place where you are going to stroll and purchase cute souvenirs – it's a bustling and frenetic market for local people. You'll find lots of exotic snacks, and a bevvy of photo opportunities.
(Jalan Bandar, Terengganu)

86. Take in the Views From Kuala Lumpur Tower

Something that dominates the skyline in the centre of Kuala Lumpur is the Kuala Lumpur Tower, a tower that as an antennae and is used for communication purposes. That might not sound all that exciting, but this is actually the 7th largest tower in the world, and it has its own observation deck and a revolving restaurant from which visitors have incredible vistas of the whole of the city.
(Jalan P Ramlee, Kuala Lumpur; www.menarakl.com.my)

87. Discover Contemporary Art at the Hin Bus Depot Art Centre

If you are the artsy type, something that you absolutely need to check out while you are in Georgetown, Penang, is the Hin Bus Depot Art Centre, an unlikely spot that is dedicated to contemporary arts on the island. This was once a bus depot, but now the large walls are dedicated to hanging up works of art and for projecting screenings of hipster art movies.

(31 Jalan Gurdwara, George Town; http://hinbusdepot.com)

88. Have a Sailfish Fishing Adventure in Kuala Rompin

If your idea of the perfect getaway involves plenty of fishing time, a trip to Malaysia will give you the chance to take your fishing to the next level. And if you've only ever fished in rivers and lakes before, you should definitely visit Kuala Rompin where you can have a go at sailfishing. The water here is so rich with fish that it's more than possible to catch multiple fish in a day, so there's a very good chance that you'll be catching your own dinner on a trip to Malasyia.

89. Visit the Ethnology Museum in Kuching

Although Borneo is best known for its incredible nature, there are also some great cultural experiences to be had there, and a morning at the Ethnology Museum in Kuching would definitely be time well spent. This is a place to learn about the city, the state, the people who live there, and their traditions. There's a huge number of cultural objects on display, including intricately carved masks, spears, woven baskets, cooking utensils, and more. *(www.museum.sarawak.gov.my)*

90. Go Back in Time at the Mari Mari Cultural Village

Malaysia is a melting pot of all different kinds of cultures, and one of the best ways to explore all of the different native cultures of the country is to pay a visit to the Mari Mari Cultural Village, located in the deep country of Sabah in Borneo. The cultural village portrays the lives of 5 different native tribes through the stunning houses that are built there, and the people who give many demonstrations in the village.

(Inanam, 88450 Kota Kinabalu, Sabah; http://marimariculturalvillage.my)

91. Sip on Plenty of Teh Tarik

If you are the kind of person who can't start the day without a hit of caffeine, you'll find that there is definitely a strong tea and coffee culture across Malaysia, although different from what you are used to at home. One of the most popular drinks is called Teh Tarik, and this is essentially strong black tea that is made with condensed milk. The result is something too sweet for some, but it's sure to give you an energy boost. You'll find it in cafes, restaurants, and even street stalls.

92. Get Close to Crocs at Crocodile Adventureland

Malaysia is a country that is home to plenty of wild animals, and some of the most magnificent, and perhaps scary, of these is the crocodile. If you would like to see crocodiles up close, make sure you etch in a visit to Crocodile Adventureland in your diary. In fact it's here that you will find the largest numbers of crocodile and alligator species gathered together in the whole world. One of the highlights in this park is the feeding centre where you can see this ferocious creatures snap their jaws across big hulks of meat.

(Taman Buaya Langkawi Mukim Air Hangat, Jalan Datai; www.porosus.com/croc)

93. Kayak Through the Mangroves of Langkawi

The island of Langkawi is one of the most visited places in Malaysia thanks to its gorgeous beaches, but that's not the beginning and end of the island, and we totally recommend exploring the mangroves here as well. One of the best way to get around the swampy mangroves is by taking a fun kayaking trip. As you kayak through, you'll have a chance of seeing monkeys, lizards, flying lemurs, frogs, and lots of tropical birds.

94. Check Out the Gua Tambun Cave Paintings

Malaysia is a country full of incredible contrasts. In Kuala Lumpur you'll find the modern side of the country, you can find all kinds of nature across Malaysia, and if you are a history buff, you can also catch glimpses of Malaysia from thousands of years ago. One of the most special places for history buffs is Ipoh, where you can find the Gua Tambun cave paintings, which date back 2000-5000 years, and depict humans, animals, fruit, geometric shapes, and abstract motifs.

(www.tambunrockart.com)

95. Dance Your Socks Off at Paint Glow Festival

The annual Paint Glow Festival, which takes place on New Year's Eve each year in Kuala Lumpur, is the biggest UV paint party in Asia, but it's also much more than that. Tonnes of music artists take to the stage, there are world class DJs pumping massive tunes, and everybody dances to the beats while completely covered in glow in the dark ultraviolet paint. Will you be there?

96. Spend the Night in a Treehouse in the Cameron Highlands

As you travel around Malaysia, you are likely to be staying in an assortment of hotels and guesthouses, but if you fancy staying somewhere that's a little bit special and something different to the mainstream, we'd love to recommend Terra's Treehouse in the beautiful Cameron

Highlands. This indigenous themed hotel is hidden deep into the rainforest, and you get to stay in charming treehouses that are built with bamboo, rattan, and palm leaves.

(Jalan Corina 1, Taman Desa Corina, Cameron Highlands; www.terrafarm.com.my)

97. Visit Penang's Spice Garden

Penang is one of the most enduringly popular tourist spots in Malaysia, and with places like the Penang Spice Garden, it's no wonder why. This spice garden is the most impressive that we have ever encountered, with over 500 species of herbs and spices growing across a gorgeous eight acre valley. Inside the spice garden, there are three well marked trails that you can take yourself, but if you want to learn more about the garden and what's inside, it's a great idea to take one of the daily tours.

(Lot 595 Mukim 2, Jalan Teluk Bahang, Teluk Bahang, 11050 George Town; http://tropicalspicegarden.com)

98. Keep Your Kids Happy at Petrosains

Travelling with kids is both wonderful and hugely frustrating. It's great to give your kids memories from foreign countries that will last a lifetime, but it's also really difficult to keep kids entertained around the clock. That's why you should know about Petrosains. This is a science discovery centre in Kuala Lumpur where everything is rally hands on, so kids actually get to have fun while they learn new things. Perhaps it will even inspire your little ones to become scientists.

(Level 4, Suria KLCC, Petronas Twin Towers, 50088 Kuala Lumpur; www.petrosains.com.my)

99. Go White Water Rafting on the Kampar River

If you are an adventurous person, it's possible to have all kinds of adventures in the wild landscapes of Malaysia, and what could be wilder than a spot of white water rafting on the Kampar River? On this river, there is a series of 14 rapids, and you have the chance to take a rafting for around 3 hours, by which time your adrenaline will be significantly raised. Do you dare?

100. Eat Malaysian Comfort Food, Roti Canai

When it comes to comforting eats, there's actually a whole lot of choice in Malaysia, but nothing makes our stomach sing with comfort quite like roti canai, which is one of the Indian influenced dishes, brought over by the Tamils, that you can find in Malaysia. This particular roti is special because it has many layers, with a flaky outside and chewy inside. When you dip this into some lentil or chicken curry, it's sheer heaven.

101. Volunteer at the Matang Wildlife Centre

There are quite a number of wildlife centres that are dedicated to helping the lives of endangered species within Malaysia. One of the most special of these is the Matang Wildlife Centre on Borneo, which is best known for its work with orangutans. And if you want to do more than just visit, it's also possible to spend some time volunteering at the centre for up to a month, which is a way of having a totally different and incredibly rewarding Malaysia experience.

(Kubah National Park Kuching, Sarawak;
https://sarawaktourism.com/attraction/matang-wildlife-centre)

Before You Go...

Thanks for reading **101 Amazing Things to Do in Malaysia & Singapore.** We hope that it makes your trip a memorable one!

Have a great trip!

Team 101 Amazing Things

Printed in Great Britain
by Amazon